50 French Dessert Recipes

By: Kelly Johnson

Table of Contents

- Crème Brûlée
- Tarte Tatin
- Madeleines
- Chocolate Soufflé
- Profiteroles
- Clafoutis
- Éclairs
- Macarons
- Mille-Feuille (Napoleon)
- Financiers
- Canelés
- Paris-Brest
- Mont Blanc
- Crêpes Suzette
- Fruit Tarts
- Galette des Rois
- Choux à la Crème
- Quatre-Quarts
- Tarte au Citron Meringuée
- Moelleux au Chocolat
- Mousse au Chocolat
- Opera Cake
- Baba au Rhum
- Panna Cotta
- Soupe de Fruits
- Fougasse Sucrée
- Flan Pâtissier
- Gâteau Basque
- Charlotte aux Fraises
- Tarte au Chocolat
- Crêpes with Nutella
- Poached Pears in Red Wine
- Meringues
- Almond Croissants
- Parisian Flan

- Pain d'épices
- Pâte à Choux
- Sablés
- Caramelized Apple Tart
- Churros with Chocolate Sauce
- Frangipane Tart
- Almond Cake
- Vacherin
- Baba au Limoncello
- Tarte Bourdaloue
- Cointreau and Orange Sorbet
- Coconut Madeleines
- French Butter Cookies
- Crème Caramel
- Lavendar Honey Ice Cream

Crème Brûlée

Ingredients:

- 2 cups heavy cream
- 1 vanilla bean (or 1 tbsp vanilla extract)
- 5 large egg yolks
- 1/2 cup granulated sugar
- 2 tbsp brown sugar (for caramelizing)

Instructions:

1. Preheat the oven to 325°F (160°C).
2. In a saucepan, heat the cream and vanilla bean (split and scraped) over medium heat until just boiling. Remove from heat and let steep for 10 minutes. If using vanilla extract, add it after removing from heat.
3. Whisk together egg yolks and granulated sugar in a bowl until smooth.
4. Gradually pour the hot cream into the egg mixture, whisking constantly.
5. Strain the mixture through a fine mesh sieve into a bowl to remove any solids.
6. Pour the custard into ramekins and place them in a baking dish. Add hot water to the baking dish to create a water bath for the ramekins.
7. Bake for 40-45 minutes, until the custard is set but still slightly wobbly in the center.
8. Cool the crème brûlée to room temperature, then refrigerate for at least 2 hours.
9. Before serving, sprinkle brown sugar on top and use a torch to caramelize the sugar until golden and crispy.

Tarte Tatin

Ingredients:

- 6-8 medium apples (such as Granny Smith or Honeycrisp)
- 1/2 cup unsalted butter
- 1 cup granulated sugar
- 1 tsp vanilla extract
- 1 sheet puff pastry
- Pinch of salt

Instructions:

1. Preheat the oven to 375°F (190°C).
2. In a large skillet (preferably cast iron), melt the butter over medium heat. Add the sugar and cook until it forms a golden caramel, about 10 minutes.
3. Peel, core, and slice the apples. Arrange them in a circular pattern on top of the caramel in the skillet.
4. Cook the apples for about 10 minutes until they start to soften and release some juice.
5. Roll out the puff pastry and drape it over the apples, tucking the edges around the fruit.
6. Transfer the skillet to the oven and bake for 25-30 minutes, or until the pastry is golden and puffed.
7. Remove from the oven and let it cool for a few minutes. Carefully flip the tart onto a serving plate.
8. Serve warm.

Madeleines

Ingredients:

- 1/2 cup unsalted butter, melted
- 3/4 cup all-purpose flour
- 1/2 cup granulated sugar
- 2 large eggs
- 1 tsp vanilla extract
- 1/2 tsp baking powder
- 1/4 tsp salt
- Zest of 1 lemon (optional)

Instructions:

1. Preheat the oven to 375°F (190°C). Grease a madeleine pan.
2. In a bowl, whisk together the flour, sugar, baking powder, and salt.
3. In another bowl, beat the eggs and vanilla extract until light and fluffy.
4. Gently fold the dry ingredients into the egg mixture, followed by the melted butter and lemon zest.
5. Spoon the batter into the madeleine pan, filling each cavity about 3/4 full.
6. Bake for 8-10 minutes, or until the edges are golden and the tops spring back when lightly touched.
7. Remove from the pan and cool on a wire rack.

Chocolate Soufflé

Ingredients:

- 4 oz dark chocolate, chopped
- 2 tbsp unsalted butter
- 1/4 cup granulated sugar (plus extra for coating)
- 3 large egg yolks
- 3 large egg whites
- 1/4 tsp cream of tartar
- 1 tsp vanilla extract
- Pinch of salt

Instructions:

1. Preheat the oven to 375°F (190°C) and butter and sugar the sides of 4 ramekins.
2. Melt the chocolate and butter together in a heatproof bowl over simmering water.
3. Beat the egg yolks with half the sugar until thick and pale. Add the melted chocolate mixture and vanilla extract.
4. In a separate bowl, beat the egg whites with the cream of tartar and remaining sugar until stiff peaks form.
5. Gently fold the egg whites into the chocolate mixture until just combined.
6. Spoon the mixture into the prepared ramekins, smoothing the tops.
7. Bake for 12-15 minutes, or until the soufflés have risen and are slightly set in the center.
8. Serve immediately with a dusting of powdered sugar.

Profiteroles

Ingredients for Choux Pastry:

- 1/2 cup unsalted butter
- 1 cup water
- 1 cup all-purpose flour
- 1/4 tsp salt
- 4 large eggs

Ingredients for Filling:

- 1 cup heavy cream
- 2 tbsp powdered sugar
- 1 tsp vanilla extract

Instructions:

1. Preheat the oven to 400°F (200°C) and line a baking sheet with parchment paper.
2. In a saucepan, bring water and butter to a boil. Add the flour and salt all at once, stirring vigorously until the mixture forms a smooth ball.
3. Remove from heat and let it cool slightly. Add the eggs one at a time, mixing well after each addition.
4. Spoon the dough into a piping bag and pipe small rounds onto the baking sheet.
5. Bake for 20-25 minutes, or until golden and puffed.
6. For the filling, whip the heavy cream with powdered sugar and vanilla until stiff peaks form.
7. Once the profiteroles have cooled, slice them in half and fill with whipped cream.
8. Serve as is, or drizzle with chocolate sauce.

Clafoutis

Ingredients:

- 1 lb fresh cherries, pitted
- 1 cup milk
- 1/2 cup all-purpose flour
- 1/4 cup granulated sugar
- 3 large eggs
- 1 tsp vanilla extract
- Pinch of salt
- Powdered sugar for dusting

Instructions:

1. Preheat the oven to 350°F (175°C) and grease a baking dish.
2. Arrange the cherries in the bottom of the dish.
3. In a bowl, whisk together the milk, flour, sugar, eggs, vanilla extract, and salt until smooth.
4. Pour the batter over the cherries.
5. Bake for 35-40 minutes, or until puffed and golden.
6. Dust with powdered sugar and serve warm.

Éclairs

Ingredients for Choux Pastry:

- 1/2 cup unsalted butter
- 1 cup water
- 1 cup all-purpose flour
- 1/4 tsp salt
- 4 large eggs

Ingredients for Filling:

- 1 cup heavy cream
- 2 tbsp powdered sugar
- 1 tsp vanilla extract

Ingredients for Glaze:

- 4 oz dark chocolate, chopped
- 2 tbsp heavy cream

Instructions:

1. Preheat the oven to 400°F (200°C) and line a baking sheet with parchment paper.
2. In a saucepan, bring water and butter to a boil. Add the flour and salt, stirring until smooth.
3. Remove from heat and let cool slightly. Add eggs one at a time, mixing well after each.
4. Pipe the dough into long strips on the baking sheet.
5. Bake for 20-25 minutes, until golden and puffed.
6. For the filling, whip the cream with powdered sugar and vanilla until stiff.
7. For the glaze, melt the chocolate and cream together.
8. Once the éclairs have cooled, slice them in half and fill with whipped cream. Drizzle with chocolate glaze.

Macarons

Ingredients:

- 1 cup powdered sugar
- 1/2 cup almond flour
- 2 large egg whites
- 1/4 cup granulated sugar
- Pinch of salt
- 1/2 tsp vanilla extract
- Filling (buttercream or ganache of choice)

Instructions:

1. Preheat the oven to 300°F (150°C) and line a baking sheet with parchment paper.
2. Sift together the powdered sugar and almond flour.
3. Whisk the egg whites with a pinch of salt until soft peaks form, then gradually add granulated sugar until stiff peaks form.
4. Gently fold in the almond flour mixture and vanilla.
5. Pipe small rounds of the mixture onto the baking sheet.
6. Let the macarons sit for 30 minutes before baking.
7. Bake for 18-20 minutes, then cool completely.
8. Fill with buttercream or ganache and sandwich together.

Mille-Feuille (Napoleon)

Ingredients:

- 1 sheet puff pastry
- 1 1/2 cups pastry cream (vanilla custard)
- Powdered sugar for dusting
- Chocolate (optional) for decoration

Instructions:

1. Preheat the oven to 400°F (200°C).
2. Roll out the puff pastry and bake according to the package instructions, until golden and puffed.
3. Once cooled, slice the pastry into three equal pieces.
4. Spread pastry cream on one layer, then top with another piece of pastry. Repeat until all layers are stacked.
5. Dust with powdered sugar and decorate with chocolate if desired.
6. Serve immediately, or chill until ready to serve.

Financiers

Ingredients:

- 1/2 cup unsalted butter
- 1/2 cup almond flour
- 1/2 cup all-purpose flour
- 1/2 cup powdered sugar
- 4 large egg whites
- 1/4 tsp vanilla extract
- Pinch of salt

Instructions:

1. Preheat the oven to 375°F (190°C) and grease financier molds.
2. Melt the butter in a saucepan until it turns golden brown, then remove from heat and set aside to cool.
3. Sift the almond flour, all-purpose flour, and powdered sugar together in a bowl.
4. In a separate bowl, whisk the egg whites until frothy.
5. Add the dry ingredients to the egg whites and mix gently, followed by the brown butter and vanilla extract.
6. Spoon the batter into the molds and bake for 12-15 minutes, or until golden brown.
7. Let cool before serving.

Canelés

Ingredients:

- 1 cup whole milk
- 1/2 cup sugar
- 1/4 cup rum
- 1 tbsp vanilla extract
- 1/2 cup all-purpose flour
- 2 large egg yolks
- 2 tbsp unsalted butter
- 1/4 tsp salt

Instructions:

1. Preheat the oven to 400°F (200°C) and grease canelé molds.
2. In a saucepan, heat the milk, sugar, and butter until melted and warm. Let it cool slightly.
3. In a bowl, whisk together the egg yolks, rum, vanilla, and salt.
4. Slowly add the warm milk mixture to the egg yolks while stirring.
5. Add the flour and mix until smooth.
6. Let the batter rest in the fridge for at least 2 hours.
7. Fill the molds about 3/4 full with batter and bake for 45-60 minutes, or until deeply golden brown and crispy on the outside.
8. Let the canelés cool and remove from molds.

Paris-Brest

Ingredients for Choux Pastry:

- 1/2 cup unsalted butter
- 1 cup water
- 1 cup all-purpose flour
- 1/4 tsp salt
- 4 large eggs

Ingredients for Filling:

- 1 cup heavy cream
- 2 tbsp powdered sugar
- 1 tsp vanilla extract
- 1/2 cup hazelnuts, chopped

Instructions:

1. Preheat the oven to 375°F (190°C) and line a baking sheet with parchment paper.
2. In a saucepan, bring water and butter to a boil. Add the flour and salt and stir until smooth. Remove from heat and let cool slightly.
3. Add the eggs one at a time, mixing after each addition until the dough is smooth and shiny.
4. Pipe the dough into a large circle on the baking sheet to form a ring.
5. Bake for 30-35 minutes, or until golden brown and puffed.
6. For the filling, whip the heavy cream with powdered sugar and vanilla until stiff peaks form.
7. Once the Paris-Brest is cooled, slice it in half and fill with the whipped cream. Sprinkle chopped hazelnuts on top.
8. Serve and enjoy!

Mont Blanc

Ingredients:

- 1 lb chestnuts, peeled
- 1 cup sugar
- 1/2 cup milk
- 1/2 cup heavy cream
- 1 tsp vanilla extract
- 1 tbsp rum (optional)

Instructions:

1. In a saucepan, cook the chestnuts with water until soft, about 30 minutes. Drain and peel them.
2. Puree the chestnuts in a food processor with sugar and milk until smooth.
3. In a separate bowl, whip the heavy cream with vanilla extract until soft peaks form.
4. Serve the chestnut puree in small cups or bowls, topping each with a dollop of whipped cream.
5. Garnish with a drizzle of rum, if desired.

Crêpes Suzette

Ingredients for Crêpes:

- 1 cup all-purpose flour
- 1 cup milk
- 2 large eggs
- 2 tbsp melted butter
- 1 tbsp sugar
- Pinch of salt

Ingredients for Sauce:

- 1/4 cup unsalted butter
- 1/4 cup sugar
- 1/4 cup orange juice
- 1/4 cup orange liqueur (like Grand Marnier)
- Zest of 1 orange

Instructions:

1. In a bowl, whisk together the flour, milk, eggs, butter, sugar, and salt to form a smooth batter.
2. Heat a non-stick pan over medium heat and lightly grease it. Pour in a small amount of batter and swirl to coat the bottom of the pan.
3. Cook until the edges lift, then flip and cook for 1 more minute. Set aside.
4. For the sauce, melt the butter in a pan over medium heat and add the sugar. Cook until caramelized, then add the orange juice, liqueur, and zest. Simmer for a few minutes.
5. Fold the crêpes into quarters and place them in the sauce. Let them soak briefly, then serve with the sauce drizzled over the top.

Fruit Tarts

Ingredients for Pastry:

- 1 1/4 cups all-purpose flour
- 1/2 cup cold unsalted butter, cubed
- 1/4 cup powdered sugar
- 1 egg yolk

Ingredients for Filling:

- 1 cup pastry cream (or whipped cream)
- Assorted fresh fruits (berries, kiwi, etc.)

Instructions:

1. Preheat the oven to 350°F (175°C) and grease tart pans.
2. For the pastry, mix the flour, butter, and powdered sugar until crumbly. Add the egg yolk and mix to form a dough.
3. Roll out the dough and press it into the tart pans. Prick the bottom with a fork.
4. Bake for 15-20 minutes, or until golden brown. Cool completely.
5. Fill the cooled tart shells with pastry cream or whipped cream.
6. Top with fresh fruits arranged in a decorative pattern.

Galette des Rois

Ingredients:

- 2 sheets puff pastry
- 1/2 cup almond meal
- 1/2 cup powdered sugar
- 1/4 cup unsalted butter, softened
- 1 large egg
- 1/2 tsp vanilla extract
- 1/4 tsp almond extract
- Pinch of salt
- 1 dried bean (for the tradition)

Instructions:

1. Preheat the oven to 375°F (190°C) and line a baking sheet with parchment paper.
2. In a bowl, mix the almond meal, powdered sugar, butter, egg, vanilla extract, almond extract, and salt to make the filling.
3. Roll out one sheet of puff pastry and spread the almond filling evenly on it, leaving a border.
4. Place the dried bean in the filling (traditionally hidden in the pie).
5. Cover with the second sheet of puff pastry, pressing the edges to seal.
6. Brush with egg wash and bake for 25-30 minutes, or until golden brown.
7. Serve warm and enjoy!

Choux à la Crème

Ingredients for Choux Pastry:

- 1/2 cup water
- 1/2 cup unsalted butter
- 1 cup all-purpose flour
- 4 large eggs
- 1/4 tsp salt

Ingredients for Filling:

- 1 cup heavy cream
- 1/4 cup powdered sugar
- 1 tsp vanilla extract

Instructions:

1. Preheat the oven to 375°F (190°C) and grease a baking sheet.
2. In a saucepan, bring water and butter to a boil. Add the flour and salt, and stir until the dough comes together and pulls away from the sides of the pan.
3. Remove from heat and let cool slightly. Add the eggs one at a time, mixing well after each addition.
4. Spoon or pipe the dough into small mounds on the baking sheet.
5. Bake for 25-30 minutes, or until puffed and golden.
6. For the filling, whip the cream with powdered sugar and vanilla until stiff peaks form.
7. Once cooled, slice the choux pastry and fill with whipped cream.

Quatre-Quarts

Ingredients:

- 1 cup all-purpose flour
- 1 cup granulated sugar
- 1 cup unsalted butter, softened
- 4 large eggs
- 1 tsp vanilla extract
- Pinch of salt

Instructions:

1. Preheat the oven to 350°F (175°C) and grease a loaf pan.
2. Cream the butter and sugar together until light and fluffy.
3. Beat in the eggs one at a time, followed by the vanilla extract.
4. Gradually add the flour and salt, mixing until combined.
5. Pour the batter into the prepared loaf pan and bake for 50-60 minutes, or until a toothpick comes out clean.
6. Let the cake cool before slicing and serving.

Tarte au Citron Meringuée (Lemon Meringue Tart)

Ingredients for the Crust:

- 1 1/4 cups all-purpose flour
- 1/2 cup unsalted butter, cubed
- 1/4 cup powdered sugar
- 1 egg yolk
- 1 tbsp cold water

Ingredients for the Lemon Filling:

- 1 cup fresh lemon juice
- 3/4 cup granulated sugar
- 3 large eggs
- 2 tbsp cornstarch
- 1/2 cup unsalted butter, cubed
- Zest of 2 lemons

Ingredients for the Meringue:

- 4 large egg whites
- 1/2 cup granulated sugar
- 1/4 tsp cream of tartar

Instructions:

1. Preheat the oven to 350°F (175°C). For the crust, combine flour, butter, powdered sugar, egg yolk, and water in a food processor. Pulse until a dough forms.
2. Press the dough into a tart pan and chill for 15 minutes. Then, bake for 10-12 minutes or until golden.
3. For the filling, whisk together lemon juice, sugar, eggs, and cornstarch in a saucepan. Cook over medium heat, whisking constantly, until thickened.
4. Remove from heat and stir in butter and lemon zest. Pour into the baked tart shell.
5. For the meringue, beat the egg whites with cream of tartar until soft peaks form. Gradually add sugar and continue beating until stiff peaks form.
6. Spread the meringue over the lemon filling and bake for 10 minutes until golden. Cool before serving.

Moelleux au Chocolat (Chocolate Lava Cake)

Ingredients:

- 1/2 cup unsalted butter
- 6 oz dark chocolate, chopped
- 1/2 cup granulated sugar
- 2 large eggs
- 2 large egg yolks
- 1/4 cup all-purpose flour
- 1/4 tsp salt

Instructions:

1. Preheat the oven to 425°F (220°C) and butter and flour 4 ramekins.
2. Melt the butter and chocolate together in a heatproof bowl over simmering water or in the microwave.
3. In a separate bowl, whisk the eggs, egg yolks, and sugar until pale and fluffy.
4. Add the melted chocolate mixture to the eggs and stir in the flour and salt.
5. Pour the batter into the ramekins and bake for 12-14 minutes, or until the edges are set but the center is soft.
6. Let the cakes cool for 1 minute, then invert onto plates. Serve warm.

Mousse au Chocolat (Chocolate Mousse)

Ingredients:

- 8 oz dark chocolate, chopped
- 2 tbsp unsalted butter
- 1 1/4 cups heavy cream
- 2 tbsp powdered sugar
- 1 tsp vanilla extract

Instructions:

1. Melt the chocolate and butter together in a heatproof bowl over simmering water or in the microwave. Let it cool slightly.
2. In a separate bowl, whip the heavy cream with powdered sugar and vanilla until soft peaks form.
3. Gently fold the whipped cream into the melted chocolate until smooth.
4. Spoon the mousse into serving glasses and refrigerate for at least 2 hours before serving.

Opera Cake

Ingredients for the Joconde Sponge:

- 3/4 cup almond flour
- 3/4 cup powdered sugar
- 4 large eggs
- 1/4 cup all-purpose flour
- 1/4 cup unsalted butter, melted
- 1/4 tsp vanilla extract

Ingredients for the Coffee Syrup:

- 1/4 cup brewed coffee
- 2 tbsp sugar
- 1 tbsp rum (optional)

Ingredients for the Buttercream:

- 1/2 cup unsalted butter, softened
- 1/4 cup powdered sugar
- 1 tbsp brewed coffee

Ingredients for the Ganache:

- 1/2 cup heavy cream
- 4 oz dark chocolate, chopped

Instructions:

1. Preheat the oven to 375°F (190°C) and grease a baking sheet.
2. For the sponge, beat the eggs with powdered sugar until thick. Fold in almond flour, flour, melted butter, and vanilla.
3. Spread the batter evenly on the sheet and bake for 10-12 minutes. Let cool.
4. For the coffee syrup, combine coffee, sugar, and rum in a saucepan. Heat until the sugar dissolves.
5. For the buttercream, whip butter with powdered sugar and coffee until smooth.
6. For the ganache, heat the cream and pour over chopped chocolate. Stir until smooth.
7. To assemble, cut the sponge into layers, brush with coffee syrup, spread buttercream, and top with ganache. Repeat layers.
8. Chill before serving.

Baba au Rhum

Ingredients for the Dough:

- 1/2 cup warm milk
- 1/4 cup sugar
- 1 tbsp active dry yeast
- 3 cups all-purpose flour
- 1/2 tsp salt
- 4 large eggs
- 1/2 cup unsalted butter, softened
- Zest of 1 lemon

Ingredients for the Syrup:

- 1 cup water
- 1/2 cup sugar
- 1/4 cup dark rum

Instructions:

1. In a bowl, combine warm milk, sugar, and yeast. Let it sit for 5 minutes to activate.
2. Mix the flour, salt, eggs, and butter in a separate bowl, then add the yeast mixture. Knead until smooth.
3. Let the dough rise in a warm place for 1 hour, or until doubled in size.
4. Preheat the oven to 350°F (175°C) and grease baba molds.
5. Divide the dough between the molds and let rise for 30 minutes.
6. Bake for 20-25 minutes, or until golden brown.
7. For the syrup, heat water and sugar in a saucepan until dissolved. Remove from heat and add rum.
8. Soak the babas in the syrup for 15 minutes before serving.

Panna Cotta

Ingredients:

- 1 1/4 cups heavy cream
- 1/4 cup sugar
- 1 tsp vanilla extract
- 1 packet gelatin
- 2 tbsp water

Instructions:

1. In a small bowl, dissolve the gelatin in water and let it bloom for 5 minutes.
2. In a saucepan, heat the cream and sugar until warm. Add the bloomed gelatin and stir until dissolved.
3. Stir in the vanilla extract.
4. Pour the mixture into serving glasses and refrigerate for at least 4 hours, or until set.
5. Serve with fresh berries or fruit compote.

Soupe de Fruits (Fruit Soup)

Ingredients:

- 2 cups mixed fresh fruit (berries, melon, apples)
- 1/2 cup fruit juice (orange, apple, or mixed)
- 1 tbsp honey
- 1 tbsp lemon juice

Instructions:

1. Chop the fruit into small pieces.
2. In a blender, combine the fruit, fruit juice, honey, and lemon juice.
3. Blend until smooth.
4. Serve chilled with a garnish of mint or a dollop of whipped cream.

Fougasse Sucrée (Sweet Focaccia)

Ingredients:

- 3 cups all-purpose flour
- 1/4 cup sugar
- 1 tsp active dry yeast
- 1 tsp salt
- 1/2 cup warm water
- 1/4 cup olive oil
- 1/2 tsp vanilla extract
- 1/4 cup candied orange peel, chopped
- 1/4 cup powdered sugar for dusting

Instructions:

1. In a bowl, combine the flour, sugar, yeast, and salt.
2. Add warm water, olive oil, and vanilla extract. Mix to form a dough.
3. Knead the dough for 10 minutes, then let rise for 1 hour.
4. Preheat the oven to 375°F (190°C) and shape the dough into a flat oval on a baking sheet.
5. Top with chopped candied orange peel and bake for 20-25 minutes, or until golden brown.
6. Dust with powdered sugar before serving.

Flan Pâtissier (French Custard Tart)

Ingredients for the Pastry:

- 1 1/4 cups all-purpose flour
- 1/4 cup sugar
- 1/2 cup unsalted butter, cubed
- 1 egg yolk
- 1 tbsp cold water

Ingredients for the Custard:

- 2 cups whole milk
- 1/2 cup sugar
- 3 large egg yolks
- 1 tsp vanilla extract
- 1/4 cup cornstarch

Instructions:

1. Preheat the oven to 375°F (190°C) and grease a tart pan.
2. For the pastry, mix the flour, sugar, and butter until crumbly. Add egg yolk and water and mix into a dough.
3. Roll out the dough and press it into the tart pan. Chill for 30 minutes.
4. For the custard, whisk the egg yolks with sugar and cornstarch. Heat the milk in a saucepan, then gradually pour it over the egg mixture.
5. Cook the custard over medium heat, whisking constantly, until thickened.
6. Pour the custard into the tart shell and bake for 35-40 minutes. Let it cool before serving.

Gâteau Basque

Ingredients for the Dough:

- 2 cups all-purpose flour
- 3/4 cup granulated sugar
- 1/2 tsp baking powder
- 1/2 tsp salt
- 1/2 cup unsalted butter, softened
- 2 large eggs
- 1 tsp vanilla extract
- 1 tbsp rum (optional)

Ingredients for the Filling:

- 1/2 cup pastry cream (store-bought or homemade)
- 1/2 cup cherry jam (or other fruit preserves)

Instructions:

1. Preheat the oven to 350°F (175°C) and grease a round cake pan.
2. For the dough, combine flour, sugar, baking powder, and salt. Add butter, eggs, vanilla extract, and rum. Mix until the dough comes together.
3. Divide the dough into two portions, one slightly larger for the base. Roll out the larger portion and line the bottom of the cake pan.
4. Spread a layer of pastry cream on the dough, followed by a layer of cherry jam.
5. Roll out the remaining dough and place it over the filling. Press the edges to seal.
6. Bake for 35-40 minutes until golden brown. Let it cool before serving.

Charlotte aux Fraises (Strawberry Charlotte)

Ingredients for the Biscuit:

- 4 large eggs
- 1/2 cup granulated sugar
- 1/2 cup all-purpose flour
- 1/2 tsp vanilla extract

Ingredients for the Filling:

- 3 cups fresh strawberries, hulled and halved
- 1 cup heavy cream
- 1/4 cup powdered sugar
- 1 tbsp lemon juice
- 1/2 packet gelatin (optional)

Instructions:

1. Preheat the oven to 350°F (175°C). Grease and line a springform pan with parchment paper.
2. For the biscuit, whisk eggs and sugar until pale and fluffy. Gently fold in the flour and vanilla extract.
3. Pour the batter into the pan and bake for 15-20 minutes until golden. Let cool and cut into strips.
4. For the filling, whip the cream with powdered sugar and lemon juice until stiff peaks form.
5. Fold in the fresh strawberries, and if desired, dissolve gelatin in a little water and mix into the filling.
6. Line the sides of the pan with biscuit strips, then pour the strawberry filling inside. Chill for at least 4 hours.
7. Serve cold and garnish with additional strawberries.

Tarte au Chocolat (Chocolate Tart)

Ingredients for the Crust:

- 1 1/4 cups all-purpose flour
- 1/4 cup cocoa powder
- 1/4 cup powdered sugar
- 1/2 cup unsalted butter, cubed
- 1 egg yolk
- 2 tbsp cold water

Ingredients for the Chocolate Filling:

- 8 oz dark chocolate
- 1 cup heavy cream
- 2 tbsp unsalted butter
- 1 tsp vanilla extract

Instructions:

1. Preheat the oven to 350°F (175°C) and grease a tart pan.
2. For the crust, combine flour, cocoa powder, and powdered sugar. Add butter, egg yolk, and water. Mix to form a dough.
3. Press the dough into the tart pan and bake for 10-12 minutes. Let cool.
4. For the filling, heat the cream in a saucepan until it begins to simmer. Pour over the chopped chocolate and stir until smooth.
5. Stir in butter and vanilla extract.
6. Pour the chocolate mixture into the cooled crust and chill for 2-3 hours until set.

Crêpes with Nutella

Ingredients for the Crêpes:

- 1 cup all-purpose flour
- 1 1/4 cups milk
- 2 large eggs
- 2 tbsp melted butter
- 1 tbsp sugar
- 1 tsp vanilla extract

Filling:

- Nutella (or chocolate spread)

Instructions:

1. In a bowl, whisk together the flour, milk, eggs, melted butter, sugar, and vanilla extract until smooth.
2. Heat a non-stick pan over medium heat and lightly grease with butter.
3. Pour a small amount of batter into the pan and swirl to spread evenly. Cook for 1-2 minutes, then flip and cook the other side for another minute.
4. Remove the crêpe and repeat with the remaining batter.
5. Spread Nutella on one side of each crêpe, fold or roll, and serve.

Poached Pears in Red Wine

Ingredients:

- 4 ripe pears, peeled and cored
- 2 cups red wine
- 1/2 cup sugar
- 1 cinnamon stick
- 2 cloves
- 1 orange, sliced

Instructions:

1. In a saucepan, combine red wine, sugar, cinnamon stick, cloves, and orange slices.
2. Bring to a simmer and stir until the sugar dissolves.
3. Add the pears to the saucepan, ensuring they are submerged in the liquid. Simmer for 20-25 minutes, or until tender.
4. Remove the pears from the wine and reduce the sauce over medium heat until thickened.
5. Serve the pears with the reduced sauce drizzled over them.

Meringues

Ingredients:

- 4 large egg whites
- 1 cup granulated sugar
- 1 tsp vanilla extract
- 1/4 tsp cream of tartar

Instructions:

1. Preheat the oven to 225°F (110°C). Line a baking sheet with parchment paper.
2. In a clean bowl, beat the egg whites with cream of tartar until soft peaks form.
3. Gradually add sugar, 1 tbsp at a time, and continue beating until stiff peaks form.
4. Fold in vanilla extract.
5. Spoon or pipe the meringue onto the prepared baking sheet in small peaks.
6. Bake for 1.5 to 2 hours until dry and crisp. Let cool completely.

Almond Croissants

Ingredients for the Almond Filling:

- 1/2 cup almond flour
- 1/4 cup powdered sugar
- 1/4 cup unsalted butter, softened
- 1 egg
- 1 tsp vanilla extract

Ingredients for the Croissants:

- 6 croissants, day-old
- 1/4 cup almond syrup (or simple syrup)
- 1/4 cup sliced almonds
- Powdered sugar for dusting

Instructions:

1. Preheat the oven to 350°F (175°C) and line a baking sheet with parchment paper.
2. For the filling, mix almond flour, powdered sugar, butter, egg, and vanilla until smooth.
3. Slice the croissants in half and spread a layer of almond filling inside.
4. Place the croissants on the baking sheet and brush with almond syrup.
5. Top with sliced almonds and bake for 10-15 minutes until golden.
6. Dust with powdered sugar before serving.

Parisian Flan

Ingredients for the Pastry:

- 1 1/4 cups all-purpose flour
- 1/2 cup unsalted butter, cubed
- 1/4 cup powdered sugar
- 1 egg yolk
- 1 tbsp cold water

Ingredients for the Custard:

- 2 1/2 cups whole milk
- 1/2 cup sugar
- 4 large eggs
- 1 tsp vanilla extract
- 1/4 cup cornstarch

Instructions:

1. Preheat the oven to 350°F (175°C) and grease a tart pan.
2. For the pastry, mix the flour, powdered sugar, butter, and egg yolk until a dough forms. Add water as needed.
3. Roll out the dough and line the tart pan. Bake for 10 minutes.
4. For the custard, whisk together milk, sugar, eggs, vanilla extract, and cornstarch. Cook in a saucepan over medium heat until thickened.
5. Pour the custard into the baked pastry shell and bake for 25-30 minutes until golden.
6. Let cool before serving.

Pain d'Épices (Spiced Honey Cake)

Ingredients:

- 1 1/2 cups all-purpose flour
- 1/2 tsp baking soda
- 1 tsp ground cinnamon
- 1/2 tsp ground ginger
- 1/4 tsp ground cloves
- 1/4 tsp salt
- 1/2 cup honey
- 1/2 cup brown sugar
- 2 large eggs
- 1/2 cup milk
- 1/4 cup unsalted butter, melted

Instructions:

1. Preheat the oven to 350°F (175°C) and grease a loaf pan.
2. In a bowl, combine flour, baking soda, cinnamon, ginger, cloves, and salt.
3. In another bowl, whisk together honey, brown sugar, eggs, milk, and melted butter.
4. Gradually add the dry ingredients to the wet ingredients and stir until combined.
5. Pour the batter into the loaf pan and bake for 40-45 minutes, or until a toothpick comes out clean.
6. Let the cake cool before slicing and serving.

Pâte à Choux

Ingredients:

- 1 cup water
- 1/2 cup unsalted butter
- 1 cup all-purpose flour
- 1/4 tsp salt
- 4 large eggs

Instructions:

1. Preheat the oven to 375°F (190°C). Line a baking sheet with parchment paper.
2. In a saucepan, bring water and butter to a boil over medium heat. Once the butter melts, add flour and salt, stirring constantly until a dough forms.
3. Continue to cook for 1-2 minutes, then remove from heat.
4. Gradually add eggs, one at a time, mixing until smooth after each addition.
5. Spoon or pipe the dough onto the prepared baking sheet in small mounds or shapes.
6. Bake for 20-25 minutes, until golden and puffed up. Let cool before filling with cream or serving.

Sablés (French Butter Cookies)

Ingredients:

- 1 1/2 cups all-purpose flour
- 1/2 cup powdered sugar
- 1/4 cup cornstarch
- 1/4 tsp salt
- 1/2 cup unsalted butter, softened
- 1 egg yolk
- 1 tsp vanilla extract

Instructions:

1. Preheat the oven to 350°F (175°C) and line a baking sheet with parchment paper.
2. In a bowl, combine flour, powdered sugar, cornstarch, and salt.
3. Add butter, egg yolk, and vanilla extract. Mix until the dough comes together.
4. Roll the dough out to 1/4-inch thickness and cut into desired shapes using a cookie cutter.
5. Place the cookies on the prepared baking sheet and bake for 12-15 minutes until lightly golden around the edges.
6. Let the cookies cool before serving.

Caramelized Apple Tart

Ingredients for the Crust:

- 1 1/4 cups all-purpose flour
- 1/2 cup unsalted butter, cubed
- 1/4 cup powdered sugar
- 1 egg yolk
- 1 tbsp cold water

Ingredients for the Filling:

- 4 medium apples, peeled, cored, and sliced thinly
- 1/2 cup sugar
- 2 tbsp butter
- 1 tsp cinnamon
- 1 tbsp lemon juice

Instructions:

1. Preheat the oven to 350°F (175°C). Grease a tart pan.
2. For the crust, mix flour, powdered sugar, and butter until it resembles crumbs. Add egg yolk and water, mixing to form a dough. Press into the tart pan and chill for 15 minutes.
3. For the filling, melt butter in a skillet over medium heat. Add apples, sugar, cinnamon, and lemon juice. Cook for 5-7 minutes until the apples soften.
4. Spread the caramelized apple mixture over the crust and bake for 20-25 minutes until golden.
5. Allow the tart to cool before serving.

Churros with Chocolate Sauce

Ingredients for the Churros:

- 1 cup water
- 2 tbsp unsalted butter
- 1 tbsp sugar
- 1/2 tsp salt
- 1 cup all-purpose flour
- 2 large eggs
- Vegetable oil for frying

Ingredients for the Chocolate Sauce:

- 4 oz dark chocolate
- 1/2 cup heavy cream
- 1 tbsp sugar

Instructions:

1. For the churros, bring water, butter, sugar, and salt to a boil in a saucepan. Stir in the flour and cook for 2-3 minutes until a dough forms.
2. Remove from heat and let it cool slightly. Beat in eggs one at a time until smooth.
3. Heat oil in a frying pan over medium heat. Spoon the dough into a piping bag with a star tip.
4. Pipe strips of dough into the hot oil and fry until golden brown. Drain on paper towels.
5. For the chocolate sauce, heat heavy cream in a saucepan until simmering. Pour over chopped chocolate and stir until smooth.
6. Serve the churros with the chocolate sauce for dipping.

Frangipane Tart

Ingredients for the Crust:

- 1 1/4 cups all-purpose flour
- 1/4 cup powdered sugar
- 1/2 cup unsalted butter, cubed
- 1 egg yolk
- 1 tbsp cold water

Ingredients for the Frangipane Filling:

- 1/2 cup almond flour
- 1/4 cup sugar
- 1/4 cup unsalted butter, softened
- 1 egg
- 1 tbsp flour
- 1 tsp vanilla extract

Instructions:

1. Preheat the oven to 350°F (175°C) and grease a tart pan.
2. For the crust, mix flour, powdered sugar, and butter until crumbly. Add egg yolk and water, mixing to form a dough. Press into the tart pan and chill for 15 minutes.
3. For the frangipane filling, beat almond flour, sugar, butter, egg, flour, and vanilla extract until smooth.
4. Spread the filling into the tart crust and bake for 25-30 minutes until golden and set.
5. Allow the tart to cool before serving.

Almond Cake

Ingredients:

- 1 1/2 cups almond flour
- 1/2 cup granulated sugar
- 1/4 cup all-purpose flour
- 1/2 tsp baking powder
- 1/4 tsp salt
- 3 large eggs
- 1/2 cup unsalted butter, melted
- 1 tsp vanilla extract

Instructions:

1. Preheat the oven to 350°F (175°C) and grease a cake pan.
2. In a bowl, combine almond flour, sugar, all-purpose flour, baking powder, and salt.
3. Beat in eggs, melted butter, and vanilla extract until smooth.
4. Pour the batter into the cake pan and bake for 25-30 minutes until a toothpick comes out clean.
5. Let the cake cool before serving. Optionally, dust with powdered sugar or serve with fresh berries.

Vacherin (Meringue and Ice Cream Dessert)

Ingredients for the Meringue:

- 4 large egg whites
- 1 cup granulated sugar
- 1 tsp vanilla extract
- 1/4 tsp vinegar

Ingredients for the Ice Cream:

- 2 cups vanilla ice cream (or any flavor of your choice)
- 1/2 cup whipped cream (optional)

Instructions:

1. Preheat the oven to 250°F (120°C) and line a baking sheet with parchment paper.
2. For the meringue, beat the egg whites with vinegar until soft peaks form. Gradually add sugar and continue to beat until stiff peaks form.
3. Spoon or pipe the meringue into circles or layers on the prepared baking sheet. Bake for 1.5-2 hours until dry and crisp. Turn off the oven and let the meringue cool completely.
4. To assemble, layer meringue discs with scoops of ice cream, alternating between the two. Top with whipped cream if desired.
5. Serve immediately or freeze for later.

Baba au Limoncello

Ingredients:

- 1 1/4 cups all-purpose flour
- 1/4 cup sugar
- 1/4 tsp salt
- 1/4 oz dry yeast
- 1/4 cup warm milk
- 3 large eggs
- 1/2 cup unsalted butter, melted
- 1/2 cup Limoncello liqueur
- 1/4 cup sugar (for syrup)

Instructions:

1. Preheat the oven to 350°F (175°C). Grease a baba mold or a bundt pan.
2. In a bowl, combine flour, sugar, salt, and yeast. Add warm milk and mix until smooth.
3. Add eggs, one at a time, mixing after each addition. Stir in melted butter.
4. Pour the batter into the prepared mold and let rise for 1 hour.
5. Bake for 20-25 minutes until golden and a toothpick comes out clean.
6. For the syrup, combine Limoncello and sugar in a saucepan over medium heat. Stir until the sugar dissolves.
7. Once the baba has cooled, pour the syrup over it, allowing it to soak in.
8. Serve with whipped cream or mascarpone if desired.

Tarte Bourdaloue

Ingredients for the Almond Cream:

- 1/2 cup almond flour
- 1/2 cup butter, softened
- 1/4 cup sugar
- 2 large eggs
- 1 tbsp all-purpose flour
- 1 tsp vanilla extract

Ingredients for the Tart:

- 1 pre-baked tart shell (9-inch)
- 3 pears, peeled, cored, and halved
- 1 tbsp lemon juice
- 1/4 cup sliced almonds

Instructions:

1. Preheat the oven to 375°F (190°C).
2. Toss the pear halves with lemon juice to prevent browning.
3. For the almond cream, beat the almond flour, butter, sugar, eggs, flour, and vanilla extract until smooth.
4. Spread the almond cream into the pre-baked tart shell.
5. Place the pear halves on top of the almond cream, slightly overlapping.
6. Sprinkle sliced almonds on top and bake for 30-35 minutes until golden and set.
7. Let the tart cool before serving.

Cointreau and Orange Sorbet

Ingredients:

- 2 cups fresh orange juice
- 1/2 cup sugar
- 1/4 cup Cointreau liqueur
- 1 tsp orange zest
- 1/2 cup water

Instructions:

1. In a saucepan, combine orange juice, sugar, and water. Heat over medium, stirring until the sugar dissolves.
2. Remove from heat and add Cointreau and orange zest. Let cool to room temperature.
3. Pour the mixture into an ice cream maker and churn according to the manufacturer's instructions.
4. Once frozen, transfer the sorbet to a container and freeze for at least 2 hours before serving.

Coconut Madeleines

Ingredients:

- 1 cup all-purpose flour
- 1/2 cup shredded coconut
- 1/4 cup sugar
- 1/4 tsp baking powder
- 1/4 tsp salt
- 1/2 cup unsalted butter, melted
- 2 large eggs
- 1 tsp vanilla extract

Instructions:

1. Preheat the oven to 350°F (175°C) and grease a madeleine pan.
2. In a bowl, combine flour, coconut, sugar, baking powder, and salt.
3. Beat the eggs and vanilla extract in a separate bowl until light and fluffy.
4. Gradually fold in the dry ingredients and melted butter until just combined.
5. Spoon the batter into the madeleine pan, filling each mold about 3/4 full.
6. Bake for 10-12 minutes, or until the madeleines are golden.
7. Let them cool slightly before serving.

French Butter Cookies

Ingredients:

- 1 1/2 cups all-purpose flour
- 1/2 cup unsalted butter, softened
- 1/4 cup powdered sugar
- 1/2 tsp vanilla extract
- 1/4 tsp salt
- 1 egg yolk

Instructions:

1. Preheat the oven to 350°F (175°C) and line a baking sheet with parchment paper.
2. Cream the butter and powdered sugar together until smooth. Add the egg yolk, vanilla extract, and salt, mixing well.
3. Gradually add the flour and mix until a dough forms.
4. Roll the dough into small balls and place them on the prepared baking sheet.
5. Press each cookie lightly with a fork or your fingers to flatten.
6. Bake for 10-12 minutes or until lightly golden around the edges.
7. Let the cookies cool before serving.

Crème Caramel

Ingredients for the Caramel:

- 1/2 cup sugar
- 2 tbsp water

Ingredients for the Custard:

- 2 cups heavy cream
- 1/2 cup milk
- 1/2 cup sugar
- 3 large eggs
- 1 tsp vanilla extract

Instructions:

1. For the caramel, combine sugar and water in a small saucepan. Cook over medium heat, swirling the pan, until it turns golden brown. Carefully pour the caramel into individual ramekins.
2. For the custard, heat cream and milk in a saucepan until just simmering.
3. In a separate bowl, whisk together sugar, eggs, and vanilla extract. Gradually pour the hot cream mixture into the egg mixture, whisking constantly.
4. Strain the custard into the ramekins over the caramel.
5. Place the ramekins in a baking dish and add hot water to the dish (about halfway up the sides of the ramekins).
6. Bake at 325°F (165°C) for 45-50 minutes, until the custard is set.
7. Let cool, then refrigerate for at least 2 hours before serving.

Lavender Honey Ice Cream

Ingredients:

- 2 cups heavy cream
- 1 cup milk
- 1/2 cup honey
- 2 tbsp dried lavender
- 4 large egg yolks
- 1 tsp vanilla extract

Instructions:

1. In a saucepan, combine cream, milk, honey, and lavender. Heat over medium until the mixture begins to simmer. Remove from heat and steep for 10 minutes.
2. Strain the mixture to remove the lavender.
3. In a separate bowl, whisk the egg yolks. Gradually add the warm cream mixture to the yolks, whisking constantly.
4. Return the mixture to the saucepan and cook over low heat, stirring until it thickens.
5. Strain the custard into a bowl, then cool to room temperature.
6. Stir in vanilla extract and refrigerate for at least 4 hours, or overnight.
7. Churn the mixture in an ice cream maker according to the manufacturer's instructions. Freeze until firm.

www.ingramcontent.com/pod-product-compliance
Lightning Source LLC
LaVergne TN
LVHW081337060526
838201LV00055B/2704